46 Sriracha Flavored Recipes

Delicious Sriracha Hot Sauce Cookbook For A Spicy Palate

By Brianne Heaton

© Revelry Publishing 2014

Copyright 2014 by Revelry Publishing

All Rights reserved under International and Pan-American Copyright Conventions. By payment of required fees, you have been granted the non-exclusive, non-transferable right to access and read the text of this book. No part of this text may be reproduced, transmitted, downloaded, decompiled, reverse-engineered or stored in or introduced into any information storage and retrieval system, in any form or by any means, whether electronic or mechanical, now known, hereinafter invented, without express written permission of the publisher.

DISCLAIMER

All information in this book has been carefully researched and checked for factual accuracy. However, the authors and publishers make no warranty, express or implied, that the information contained herein is appropriate for every individual, situation or purpose, and assume no responsibility for errors or omissions. The reader assumes the risk and full responsibility for all actions, and the authors will not be held responsible for any loss or damage, whether consequential, incidental, special or otherwise that may result from the information presented in this publication.

We have relied on our own experience as well as many different sources for this book, and we have done our best to check facts and to give credit where it is due. In the event that any material is incorrect or has been used without proper permission, please contact us so that the oversight can be corrected.

ISBN-13: 978-1987863024
ISBN-10: 198786302X

Other books by Brianne Heaton:

<u>51 Dump Cake Recipes: Scrumptious Dump Cake Desserts To Satisfy Your Sweet Tooth</u>

Baking does not have to be difficult or intimidating. You can make a delicious cake in just a few steps, with just a few ingredients by using a "dump" cake recipe. Dump cakes make less mess than traditional cakes and offer unusual and decadent choices that will wow those fortunate enough to have a bite.

<u>56 Breakfast Sandwich Recipes: Irresistible Sandwich Ideas to Kickstart Your Morning</u>

Breakfast is the most important meal of the day so it makes sense to treat it so. Are you finding it difficult to get the right balance and variety of taste experiences every day? With breakfast sandwich mania in full swing, there is no shortage of breakfast ideas here.

<u>50 Holiday Dessert Recipes: Delectable Dessert Ideas For The Christmas Holidays And Other Special Occasions</u>

Wow your family and friends with the most decadent cakes, creamiest cheesecakes, most delicious cookies, juiciest pies and most interesting international desserts! It's time to bring the baker in you to the surface and make the best desserts ever! Indulge in these holiday delights with the confidence of having made it yourself!

<u>51 Easter Dessert Ideas: Scrumptious Easter Recipes For Any Occasion</u>

This holiday cookbook collection of 51 Easter dessert recipes has something tasty and enticing for everyone, and you don't have to be Julia Child in order to pull them off. The recipes can also be used for other special occasions.

Get the latest update on new releases from the author at:

htttps://www.brianneheaton.com/newsletter

Table of Contents

Introduction 1
Seven-Day Sriracha Meal Plan 2
Seven-Day Sriracha Meal Plan Shopping List 4
Daily Fresh Purchases 6

Breakfast 11
   1 - Turkey & Chorizo Breakfast Hash 13
   2 - Jalapeno Corn Waffles with Jalapeno And Maple Sriracha Syrup 15

Appetizers 17
   3 - Grilled Lemongrass Shrimp 19
   4 - Sriracha Ketchup and Taro Fries 21
   5 - Garlic Sriracha Wings 22
   6 - Scallops With Sriracha Beurre Blanc 24
   7 - Festive Shrimp Cocktail 26
   8 - Sriracha Quinoa Cheese Bites 28
   9 - Grilled Sriracha Turkey Meatballs 29
   10 - Spicy Grilled Shrimp 31

Main Dishes 33
   11 - Thai Spicy Sauce with Chicken 35
   12 - Sriracha and Peanut Butter-Glazed Salmon 36
   13 - Ginger Creamed Tuna with Sesame-Crust 37
   14 - Sriracha Molasses BBQ Pork Ribs 39
   15 - Sriracha Spaghetti Squash with Turkey 41
   16 - Sweet Sriracha Skewered Beef 42
   17 - Sriracha Black Bean Burger 43
   18 - Sriracha Veggie Fried Rice 45

Vegetarian And Salads 47
   19 - Spicy Mayo Fried Sole Sandwiches 49
   20 - Orange Broccoli and Tofu 50
   21 - Sriracha Tofu Skewers 51
   22 - Thai Style Kale and Carrot Salad 52
   23 - Roasted Sriracha Cauliflower 53

24 - Cauliflower Quinoa Medley with Sriracha Almond Sauce... 54
25 - Sriracha Zest Roasted Chickpeas 56

Soups And Stews 57
26 - Sriracha Honey Beef Stew 59
27 - Egg with Mushroom Shrimp Noodle Soup 61
28 - Coconut Chicken Soup 63
29 - Sriracha Black Bean Soup 64
30 - Sriracha Beef Stew 66
31 - Sriracha Garlic Butternut Squash & Pumpkin Soup............. 67

Desserts... 69
32 - Sriracha Choco Popsicles.. 71
33 - Crunchy Pecan Sriracha Brownies.. 73
34 - Lime Sriracha Donuts 75
35 - Sriracha Ice Cream Sandwich Delight..................................... 77
36 - Chocolate Bite Ice Cream 79
37 - Crispy Sriracha Peach Bake 81
38 - Spiced Lattice Apple Pie 82

Specialty Sauces 85
39 - Mayonnaise with Sriracha 87
40 - Creamy Lime Sriracha Dip 88
41 - Asian Bean Dip 89

Drinks... 91
42 - Sriracha Bloody Mary 93
43 - Sriracha Strawberry Margarita 94
44 - Spicy Pineapple Paradise 95
45 - Mango Sriracha Shots 96
46 - Ginger Sriracha Lime Cocktail 97

Thank You 98
Other Books by Brianne Heaton.. 99
About the Author – Brianne Heaton.. 100
Connect with Brianne Heaton 101

Introduction

Want to turn up the heat on your buffalo wings? Add a little Sriracha. Think your potato soup is a little too bland? Sprinkle in some Sriracha. Planning on making an authentic Vietnamese pho soup? It's not done until you add the Sriracha.

It's no secret: Sriracha is everywhere! The green-capped hot sauce has become a household name since its inception in the 1980s, and no other hot sauce can compare. This unique blend of hybrid jalapeño peppers, garlic, vinegar, salt, and sugar brings serious attention to any dinner, dessert, and even drink recipe.

What makes Sriracha different from those other brands? Fresh chilies! While other hot sauces use dried chilies, which are often easier to produce and make into hot sauce, Sriracha has only ever used fresh chilies.

Check out these delectable dessert, appetizer, entree, and drink recipes and see how Sriracha can enrich even the dullest of meals. Follow our meal plan for a whole week full of delicious Sriracha meals. Your taste buds will thank you for it.

Seven-Day Sriracha Meal Plan

Appetizer, Main Dish, Soup or Salad and Dessert

Day 1

- Appetizer - Festive Shrimp Cocktail
- Side - Sriracha Zest Roasted Chickpeas
- Main - Sriracha Molasses BBQ Pork Ribs
- Dessert - Spiced Lattice Apple Pie

Day 2

- Appetizer - Spicy Grilled Shrimp
- Side - Cauliflower Quinoa Medley with Sriracha Almond Sauce
- Main - Sriracha Black Bean Burger
- Dessert - Sriracha Ice Cream Sandwich Delight

Day 3

- Appetizer - Sriracha Ketchup and Taro Fries
- Side - Coconut Chicken Soup
- Main - Sriracha Veggie Fried Rice
- Dessert - Lime Sriracha Donuts

Day 4

- Appetizer - Grilled Lemongrass Shrimp
- Side - Thai Style Kale and Carrot Salad
- Main - Sriracha Beef Stew
- Dessert - Crunchy Pecan Sriracha Brownies

Day 5

- Appetizer - Sriracha Quinoa Cheese Bites
- Side - Egg with Mushroom Shrimp Noodle Soup
- Main - Spicy Mayo Fried Sole Sandwiches
- Dessert - Sriracha Choco Popsicles

Day 6

- Appetizer - Scallops With Sriracha Beurre Blanc
- Side - Roasted Sriracha Cauliflower
- Main - Sriracha Honey Beef Stew
- Dessert - Crispy Sriracha Peach Bake

Day 7

- Appetizer - Garlic Sriracha Wings
- Side - Sriracha Garlic Butternut Squash & Pumpkin Soup
- Main - Sriracha and Peanut Butter-Glazed Salmon
- Dessert - Chocolate Bite Ice Cream

Seven-Day Sriracha Meal Plan Shopping List

This shopping list is designed to help you plan your meal for each day and to make it as easy as possible in terms of stocking your 'dry' cupboard items, rather than shopping every day for them. All other ingredients are listed per day, other than freezer items, which are pretty negligible in terms of quantities. Where a product is listed several times, always check how much you have left – the quantities are purely an example.

Store Cupboard

Dried Herbs and Spices (where fresh may not be appropriate or dried is more suitable)

Condiments

Salt, sea salt, garlic powder, black pepper, white pepper, Old Bay seasoning, cloves, cinnamon, ginger powder, onion powder, cumin, chili powder.

Sauces and Oils

Sriracha sauce, clarified butter, bacon fat, vegetable oil, extra virgin olive oil, sesame oil, chili oil, peanut oil, canola oil, Worcestershire sauce, ketchup, cider vinegar, rice vinegar, fish sauce, low-sodium soy sauce, chili garlic sauce, oyster-flavored sauce.

Baking Products

Unsalted butter, regular butter, white sugar, brown sugar, powdered sugar, almond butter, smooth peanut butter, crunchy peanut butter, all-purpose flour, maple syrup, panko, baking soda, vanilla extract, chocolate chunks, baking powder, cocoa powder, bittersweet chocolate, honey, bread crumbs, cornstarch, semisweet chocolate chips, rolled oats.

Canned or Jarred Goods/Cartons

Bread-and-butter pickles, coconut milk, horseradish, chickpeas, tomato paste, molasses, low-sodium chicken stock, vegetable broth, black beans.

Frozen

Peas, pearl onions

Daily Fresh Purchases

Day 1

- 1 lemon
- 30 raw shrimp
- 2 limes
- 1 bunch fresh cilantro
- 1 rack of pork ribs (3-4 pounds or 1,350-1,800 g)
- 1 onion
- Crust for 2 crust pie
- 10 large apples

Day 2

- 8 garlic cloves
- 1 pound (450 g) large shrimp (16 to 20 count)
- ½ cup quinoa
- 1 head of cauliflower
- 5 large leaves of collard greens
- 2 teaspoon ginger root
- 1 red onion
- ½ cup minced cilantro
- 1 red pepper
- 1 green pepper
- 3 large eggs
- Lettuce
- Tomato
- Provolone cheese slices
- Ciabatta Rolls
- ¼ cup non-fat plain Greek yogurt
- ¾ cup shredded coconut
- 1 bunch of Thai basil
- 1 carton of vanilla bean ice cream

Day 3

- 1 large taro root

- 8 limes
- 6 ounces (168 g) boneless, skinless chicken breasts
- 2 pieces ginger
- cilantro leaves
- Rice
- 1 clove garlic
- 2 scallions
- 12 fresh shiitake mushrooms
- ¾ cup heavy cream
- 2 large eggs

Day 4

- 1 pound (450 g) tiger prawn or jumbo prawn
- 1 bunch lemongrass
- 4 garlic cloves
- 1 small calamansi or lime
- 1 bunch cilantro leaves
- 3 pieces of ginger
- Almond milk
- 2 bunches Tuscan kale
- 4 large carrots
- ¼ cup sesame seeds
- 2 pounds (900 g) stew beef
- 1 red bell pepper
- 1 green bell pepper
- 1 sweet onion
- 1 cup pecans
- 4 large eggs

Day 5

- 1 bunch cilantro
- ¾ cup Gruyere cheese
- Quinoa
- 3 garlic cloves
- 5 green onions

- 6 eggs
- 1 piece ginger
- 8 ounces (224 g) rice noodles
- 12 ounces (360 ml) mushrooms
- 2 cups cooked shrimp
- 1 thinly sliced jalapeño
- 2 limes
- 1 cup baby arugula
- 1 lemon
- 1 baguette
- 3 fillets Dover sole
- 1 cup Vegenaise
- Whole milk

Day 6

- 2 lemons
- 12 sea scallops
- 1 shallot
- Fresh herbs such as chives, thyme or parsley
- 5 garlic cloves
- 1 head of cauliflower
- 1 cup dried mushrooms
- 2 pounds (900 g) stew beef
- 1 piece ginger root
- 1 medium red onion
- 4 medium carrots
- 3 pounds (1,350 g) or 4-6 fresh peaches

Day 7

- ¼ cup chopped peanuts
- 3 pounds (1,350 g) chicken wings
- 8 garlic cloves
- 1 scallion
- ½ cup 1% milk
- ½ cup half-n-half cream
- 1 cup of canned pumpkin puree

- 1 pound (450 g) butternut squash
- 1 sweet onion
- 2 stalks of celery
- 1 piece of ginger
- 1 orange
- 1 bunch cilantro leaves
- 6 x 6-ounce (170 g each) salmon filets
- 1 lime

Delicious Sriracha Hot Sauce For A Spice Palate

Breakfast

Delicious Sriracha Hot Sauce For A Spice Palate

1 - Turkey & Chorizo Breakfast Hash

Ingredients:

- Salt and freshly ground black pepper
- Sriracha to taste
- 1 tablespoon chili sauce
- 2 tablespoons vegetable oil or turkey fat
- ½ cup heavy cream
- 6 ounces (168 g) fresh Mexican chorizo
- 2 cups roasted turkey meat, white and dark meat, diced into ¼-inch (0.6-cm) pieces
- 2 cups thinly sliced Brussels sprouts, raw or cooked
- 2 minced of garlic cloves
- 1 medium diced onion
- 1 large russet potato, cooked, diced into ¼-inch (0.6 cm) pieces
- 3 or 4 eggs

Directions:

1. Heat up the oil in a cast iron skillet over a medium-high heat.
2. Toss in the chorizo, then break it up with a spoon.
3. Toss in the onion, garlic, Brussels sprouts, and potato.
4. Cook everything together while stirring on occasion.
5. When the onions appear translucent and the potatoes have a brownish color, add the turkey meat, heavy cream, chili sauce, and a bit of salt and pepper.
6. Stir altogether until properly mixed.
7. Firmly press the mixture into the bottom of the pan with a rubber spatula and continue to cook.
8. A crust should form around the edges. Once it does, scrape it up and mix it all together again. Then press it all down like before.
9. Repeat the process until the crusty bites appear evenly mixed throughout the pan. This should take about 10 minutes.
10. Indent three or four wells in the hash. This will be contingent on how big the pan is.

11. Crack an egg into each well.
12. Cover the pan and let the eggs cook until they reach the softness or hardness desired.
13. Swirl in a bit of Sriracha then serve with some cranberry sauce.

2 - Jalapeno Corn Waffles with Jalapeno And Maple Sriracha Syrup

Ingredients:

For the Waffles
- ½ teaspoon salt
- 1 teaspoon baking powder
- 1 tablespoon brown sugar
- 1 tablespoon canola oil
- ¼ cup cheddar cheese
- ½ cup flour
- ½ cup corn kernels
- ½ cup melted butter
- 1 cup whole milk
- 1 cup fine yellow corn meal
- 1 large chopped jalapeno with stem and seeds removed
- 1 egg

For the Syrup
- 1 teaspoon Sriracha
- ¼ cup real maple syrup

Directions:

1. Turn on the waffle iron and let it heat up.
2. Get out a bowl and mix salt, baking powder, brown sugar, cheese, flour, corn, corn meal and jalapeno.
3. In another bowl, combine the oil, melted butter, milk and egg ensuring it is well mixed.
4. Make an indent in the dry ingredients to create a well and pour in the wet ingredients.
5. Mix it all together so the mix looks just barely combined.
6. Follow the instructions on the waffle iron for cooking steps.
7. Combine the maple syrup with the Sriracha and serve altogether.

Delicious Sriracha Hot Sauce For A Spice Palate

Appetizers

Delicious Sriracha Hot Sauce For A Spice Palate

3 - Grilled Lemongrass Shrimp

Ingredients:

- 1 pound (450 g) tiger prawn or jumbo prawn
- 6 skewers (if using bamboo, soak in water first before using)
- Oil for brushing

For the Marinade
- 1 teaspoon Sriracha
- 1 tablespoon powdered sugar
- 2 tablespoons fish sauce
- 1 grated lemongrass (use the white part only)
- 1 finely minced garlic clove

For the Chili Dipping Sauce (optional)
- 1 small calamansi, juice extracted (or 1 wedge lime)
- ½ tablespoon chopped cilantro leaves
- 1 tablespoon water
- 1½ tablespoons chili garlic sauce

Directions:

1. Ensure the shrimp are peeled and deveined but keep the tails intact.
2. Wash the shrimp in cold water. Use paper towel to dry it off and then set in a bowl.
3. Now combine all ingredients with the shrimp to create the marinade.
4. Mix well in order to coat the shrimp and let it sit for 15 minutes.
5. Carefully thread about 3 shrimp onto each of the skewers and brush the shrimp with oil.
6. Grill both sides until they appear charred and cooked entirely.
7. Serve with the optional dipping sauce.

4 - Sriracha Ketchup and Taro Fries

Ingredients:

- 2 x 1 drop chili oil
- 1 teaspoon Sriracha
- 1 teaspoon sesame oil
- 2 tablespoon ketchup
- 1 tablespoon vegetable oil
- 1 large taro root

Directions:

1. Set the oven to 400°F (200°C) degrees.
2. After washing the taro root, peel it and slice it carefully into thin strips.
3. Mix vegetable oil, sesame oil, and one drop of chili oil in a bowl.
4. Drop in the taro strips and sprinkle salt and pepper to taste.
5. Get out a cookie sheet and lay the strips on it.
6. Pop it into the oven and let them bake for 10 minutes. Flip them over and let them cook for another 10 minutes.
7. Take them out once crispy and golden.
8. Mix ketchup, Sriracha, and one drop of chili oil in a bowl for dipping.
9. Serve the strips hot with the Sriracha ketchup.

5 - Garlic Sriracha Wings

Ingredients:

- 2 tablespoons honey
- 2 tablespoons sesame oil
- ¼ cup low-sodium soy sauce
- ¼ cup chopped peanuts (optional)
- ¼ cup Sriracha
- ½ cup ketchup
- 3 pounds (1,350 g) chicken wings
- 5 minced garlic cloves
- 1 scallion, green parts chopped or thinly sliced

Directions:

1. Marinate the wings by combining honey, sesame oil, soy sauce, Sriracha, ketchup and garlic in a large bowl.
2. Get out a large freezer bag and set the wings and drummettes inside then pour the mixture in the bowl over it.
3. Seal the bag and shake it to coat the chicken. Set it on the counter for 3 hours or overnight, if preferred.

4. Once the chicken is about done marinating, set the oven to 375°F (190°C) and line a baking sheet with parchment paper or foil.
5. Put the wings on the baking sheet and put it in the oven for 25 to 30 minutes.
6. The wings are done with they appear a golden brown. Take them out and put them on a plate.
7. Top with chopped peanuts and scallions if desired.

6 - Scallops With Sriracha Beurre Blanc

Ingredients:

For the Scallops
- Salt and pepper
- 1 lemon, sliced into wedges
- 3 tablespoons clarified butter, bacon fat or vegetable oil
- 12 sea scallops

For Sriracha Beurre Blanc
- Salt and pepper
- 1 shallot, minced
- 1 tablespoon lemon juice
- 1 tablespoon Sriracha
- 2 tablespoons of chopped fresh herbs such as chives, thyme or parsley for garnish
- ¼ pound (112.5 g) of cold unsalted butter, cut into ½-inch (1.25 cm) cubes
- ½ cup rice wine vinegar (or red-wine vinegar)

Directions:

1. For the scallops, get out a large steel or cast iron skillet and set the heat to medium-high.
2. Spoon 1 tablespoon of clarified butter over scallops and add salt and pepper to taste.
3. After the pan heats up, toss in the rest of the butter and then the scallops.
4. Spread them out so they sear but not steam.
5. Cook them for about 3 minutes per side. Do not move them while on each side.
6. The finished scallop should be firm yet yielding to slight pressure.
7. Set the scallops on a warm plate for 2 to 3 minutes. Serve them up with the Sriracha beurre blanc.

8. For the Sriracha beurre blanc, take out a medium sized saucepan and toss in the lemon juice, vinegar and minced shallot.
9. Set the heat to medium.
10. The final product should be syrupy and reduced to a volume of 2 tablespoons.
11. After it is reduced, mix the Sriracha in and turn the heat to the lowest setting.
12. Use a whisk to carefully mix in the butter cubes until uniform.
13. Turn off the heat to keep the sauce from separating.
14. Sprinkle in pepper and salt if needed.
15. Serve with the scallops and garnish with chopped herbs.

7 - Festive Shrimp Cocktail

Ingredients:

For the Brine
- ¼ cup salt
- ¼ cup sugar
- 1 cup water
- 2 cups ice

For the Shrimp
- Juice from 1 lemon
- Old Bay seasoning
- 1 tablespoon olive oil
- 2-3 teaspoons Sriracha
- 30 raw, tail on shrimp

For the Cocktail Sauce
- Pinch salt
- Dash of Worcestershire sauce
- Juice from ½ lime

- 2-3 teaspoons Sriracha
- 1-2 tablespoon prepared horseradish
- 1 cup ketchup

Directions:

1. Ensure the shrimp are peeled and deveined but keep the tails intact.
2. Mix all of the brine ingredients together in a bowl and put the cleaned shrimp in. Set it in the refrigerator for 20 to 25 minutes.
3. Preheat a baking sheet under an oven broiler for about 5 minutes.
4. Take out the shrimp and drain the bowl.
5. Mix shrimp with olive oil, Sriracha, and lemon juice in a large bowl and top with Old Bay seasoning, if desired.
6. Set the shrimp out on the heated baking sheet and put it back in the broiler for about 90 seconds.
7. Flip the shrimp with tongs and broiler for another 60 to 90 seconds.
8. Take out the shrimp and put them on a cold plate.
9. Put it in the refrigerator.
10. Mix the cocktail sauce while adjusting to taste.
11. Keep both in the refrigerator until ready to eat.

8 - Sriracha Quinoa Cheese Bites

Ingredients:

- ½ teaspoon salt
- 1 tablespoon cilantro, chopped
- 1 tablespoon honey
- 1½ tablespoons Sriracha
- ½ cup bread crumbs (whole wheat or white)
- ¾ cup grated Gruyere cheese
- 2 cups cooked quinoa
- 1 minced garlic clove
- 2 thinly sliced green onions
- 2 beaten eggs

Directions:

1. Set the oven to 350°F (180°C).
2. Grease the cups of two mini 12 count muffin pans with oil and set it to the side.
3. Combine all ingredients in a bowl and mix together.
4. When the mixture becomes sticky, it's done.
5. Add more bread crumbs if it's not sticking together.
6. Scoop out the mixture and put it into the cups. Use your fingers to press it down and fill the cups to the top. There should be enough to fill 18 to 20 cups.
7. Put in the oven and bake for 15 to 20 minutes.
8. At the halfway mark, pull out the pans and rotate them.
9. Once the edges are golden, take out and let cool for 5 minutes before removing them to the cooling rack.
10. Serve right away.

9 - Grilled Sriracha Turkey Meatballs

Ingredients:

- 1 teaspoon sea salt
- 1 tablespoon finely minced garlic
- 1 tablespoon finely minced fresh ginger root
- 2-3 tablespoons Sriracha
- ½ cup whole wheat bread crumbs
- 1½ pounds (675 g) ground turkey
- 1 egg, beaten
- 3 green onions, sliced and then finely chopped
- Additional sliced green onions for garnishing

Directions:

1. Get the grill going at a medium or high heat.
2. If cooking meatballs directly on grill, spray it with non-stick spray or brush oil over the grates before heating.
3. If using a grill grid pad, spray with non-stick spray or oil and preheat grill for 5 minutes prior to cooking.

4. Chop the green onions, ginger and garlic into fine slices.
5. In a bowl, combine bread crumbs, egg, ground turkey, chopped green onions, chopped ginger, chopped garlic, salt and Sriracha.
6. Using your hands, mix everything thoroughly.
7. Measuring out about 2 tablespoons each, pack meatballs with hands and set them on grill or grid pad to cook.
8. Turn them over every 5 to 7 minutes so all sides become evenly browned.
9. Meatballs should be done within 30 minutes.
10. Serve immediately with sliced green onions if desired.

10 - Spicy Grilled Shrimp

Ingredients:

- 4 to 5 pressed garlic cloves
- ¼ teaspoon salt
- 2 teaspoons sugar
- 2 tablespoons Sriracha
- 2 tablespoons olive oil
- 1 pound (450 g) large shrimp (16 to 20 count)

Directions:

1. Ensure the shrimp are peeled and deveined but keep the tails intact.
2. Open a resealable bag and pour all the marinade ingredients inside.
3. Once mixed, toss in the shrimp and let it marinate for at least 20 minutes up to 2 hours.
4. On a skewer, slide on the shrimp and grill them until they look brown.
5. If the skewers are wood, be sure to soak them first.

- *Tip: Prepare the shrimp several hours before needed and keep them covered under a cookie sheet in the fridge.

Delicious Sriracha Hot Sauce For A Spice Palate

Main Dishes

Delicious Sriracha Hot Sauce For A Spice Palate

11 - Thai Spicy Sauce with Chicken

Ingredients:

- ½ teaspoon Asian fish sauce
- 2 teaspoons sugar
- 2 teaspoons Sriracha
- 2 tablespoons chopped cilantro
- 4 teaspoons lime juice
- ⅓ cup natural peanut butter
- 4 x 6-ounce (170 g each) boneless skinless chicken breasts, cut into 2-inch (5 cm) pieces
- 1 cup low-sodium chicken stock
- 2 smashed garlic cloves
- 4 x 1-inch (2.5 cm) slices of ginger
- Lime wedges

Directions:

1. Get out a deep 10-inch (25 cm) skillet and add the chicken, stock, ginger and garlic.
2. Let it simmer covered for 8 to 10 minutes. Be sure to skim off foam as it forms.
3. Use tongs to take out the chicken and put it in a bowl, which should be kept warm.
4. Now boil the remaining stock until only about ⅔ cup remains.
5. Put the remaining ginger and garlic in a blender with everything else except the cilantro.
6. Pour the cooking liquid into the blender through a fine mesh sieve.
7. Pour in any additional liquid from the chicken, then blend.
8. Once it is smooth, add salt if desired and pour the sauce over the chicken.
9. Top with cilantro.

12 - Sriracha and Peanut Butter-Glazed Salmon

Ingredients:

- 1 teaspoon minced fresh ginger
- 1 tablespoon rice vinegar
- 1 tablespoon fresh orange juice
- 1 heaping tablespoon Sriracha
- ¼ cup chopped cilantro leaves
- ¼ cup peanut butter
- 6 x 6-ounce (170 g each) salmon filets
- Juice from 1 lime
- Salt and pepper to taste

Directions:

1. Set the oven to 450°F (230°C).
2. Combine all the wet ingredients and cilantro in a bowl and mix together.
3. Get out a baking sheet and line it with foil.
4. Set the salmon filets fresh-side up and season with salt and pepper.
5. Scoop the glaze over the salmon to coat them.
6. Place the baking sheet in the oven for 12 to 15 minutes.
7. They're finished when they're firm to the touch. Be sure to check every two minutes if the filets are not done after the initial test.
8. Take out the filets and let them cool for a few minutes.
9. Plate the filets and serve with a pile of rice combined with green onions, lime zest, and cilantro.

13 - Ginger Creamed Tuna with Sesame-Crust

Ingredients:

- 1 tablespoon Sriracha
- 2 tablespoons mirin
- 2 tablespoons dry white wine
- ¼ cup rice vinegar
- ¼ cup fresh orange juice
- ¼ cup vegetable oil
- ½ cup thinly sliced peeled ginger
- ½ cup sesame seeds
- 6 x 6-ounce (170 g) 1-inch-thick (2.5 cm) tuna steaks
- 1½ cups heavy cream
- 2 thinly sliced garlic cloves
- ½ small onion, finely chopped
- Salt and freshly ground pepper

Directions:

1. Get out a sauce pan and set it on the stove.
2. Over a medium heat, pour 2 tablespoons of oil.
3. Toss in the ginger, onion, and garlic. Let them cook until all ingredients have softened.
4. Now toss in the vinegar, orange juice, mirin, wine, and Sriracha.
5. Keep the mixture simmering.
6. Once the liquid is nearly evaporated, pour in the cream and cut the heat in half.
7. Cook for 15 more minutes then strain the sauce.
8. Add salt and pepper. Keep the sauce warm.
9. Sprinkle salt and pepper on the tuna and season both sides with sesame seeds.
10. Get out another skillet and add the last 2 tablespoons of oil.

11. Lay the tuna in the skillet and cook over a higher heat, flipping the tuna once.
12. The tuna is done when it appears medium-rare and the sesame seeds look browned.
13. Now cut the tuna into ⅓-inch (0.8 cm) thick slices and plate with ginger cream.

14 - Sriracha Molasses BBQ Pork Ribs

Makes 4 servings

Ingredients:

- 1 teaspoon salt
- 1 teaspoon pepper
- 1 tablespoon tomato paste
- 1 tablespoon Worcestershire sauce
- 1 tablespoon molasses
- 2 tablespoons Sriracha
- 2 tablespoons brown sugar
- ¼ cup cider vinegar
- 1 cup ketchup
- 1 cup low-sodium chicken stock
- 1 rack of pork ribs (3-4 pounds or 1,350-1,800 g)
- 1 onion, diced

Directions:

1. Take out the pork and thoroughly clean and trim it. Leave just a bit of fat.
2. Once done, pat dry using paper towels. Set all meat aside.
3. Turn on the grill.
4. Move all coals to one side if using charcoal, or turn on only one side of a gas grill.
5. Clean the grill once it is preheated. To make it non-stick, use a paper towel dipped in vegetable oil and run it along the grates.
6. To mix the Sriracha BBQ sauce, get out a small saucepan.
7. Toss in the onions drizzled with oil and cook over a medium heat.
8. As soon as the onions look translucent, toss in the tomato paste and let it all cook together for a few minutes.
9. As the paste turns darker, add the remaining ingredients and whisk everything together.
10. Turn the heat up to get a boil and then bring it down to simmer for 15 minutes. Stir on occasion.

11. Use a brush to coat the ribs and place them on the cool part of the grill, meatier side down.
12. Cover the grill and let it cook for about 2 to 3 hours. Be sure to flip every 30 minutes. Brush with more sauce on each flip.
13. When the meat begins to separate from the bone, the ribs are just about done. Take them off the grill and let them rest.
14. Now bring the sauce back up to a boil to reheat it. Turn the heat down to a simmer for about 5 minutes after boiling.
15. Pour the sauce through a fine mesh strainer.
16. Let cool and then eat with ribs.

- If a grill is unavailable, slow-cook the ribs in the oven at 250°F (130°C).

15 - Sriracha Spaghetti Squash with Turkey

Makes 4 to 6 servings

Ingredients:

- 3 teaspoons fish sauce
- 2 tablespoons olive oil
- 3 tablespoons Sriracha
- 1 pound (450 g) ground turkey
- 1 medium spaghetti squash
- 1 minced medium onion
- 2 minced garlic cloves

Directions:

1. Set the oven to 375°F (190°C).
2. Grease a sheet pan using 1 tablespoon of olive oil.
3. Cut the spaghetti squash in half going lengthwise. It is best to use the tip of a sharp knife when cutting.
4. Spoon the seeds and strands into the trash and set them on the sheet, cut-side down.
5. Put the pan in the oven and let it bake for 45 minutes.
6. When the flesh of the squash comes off easily, it's done.
7. Use a fork to remove the spaghetti from the shells.
8. Put the pan off to the side.
9. Get out a large pan and heat more oil.
10. Toss in onions and garlic and let them cook until they appear translucent.
11. Toss in ground turkey to cook for 5 minutes.
12. Once browned, pour in fish sauce and Sriracha and mix evenly.
13. When the turkey appears done, add the spaghetti squash to it and mix until all components are evenly hot.
14. Serve with additional sauces if desired.

16 - Sweet Sriracha Skewered Beef

Makes 4 servings

Ingredients:

- ¼ teaspoon ground cinnamon
- ½ teaspoon salt
- 1 teaspoon ground cumin
- 1 tablespoon low-sodium soy sauce
- 2 tablespoons vegetable or canola oil
- 3 tablespoons honey
- 3 tablespoons Sriracha hot sauce
- 1 pound (450 g) top sirloin beef, cut into 1-inch (2.5 cm) cubes
- ½ cup sour cream (optional)
- 1 whole Boston lettuce (optional)
- 1 whole cucumber, cut into $1/8$-inch (0.3 cm) slices (optional)
- 1 whole lime (optional)
- 8 skewers

Directions:

1. In a bowl, mix all ingredients, then add the beef to marinate.
2. Set the bowl in the refrigerator.
3. If the skewers used are wooden, let them soak for 30 minutes or more.
4. Distribute the beef on the skewers evenly and cook to temperature desired using a skillet or grill.
5. Plate skewers with sour cream, lettuce, cilantro and sliced cucumbers mixed with the juice of one lime.

17 - Sriracha Black Bean Burger

Ingredients:

For the Burgers
- ½ teaspoon onion powder
- 1 teaspoon cumin
- 1 teaspoon chili powder
- 2 tablespoons red onion, diced
- ¼ cup minced cilantro
- ⅓ cup diced roasted red peppers
- 1 cup panko
- 1 cup diced green peppers
- 16-ounce can of black beans, rinsed
- 1 egg
- 3 garlic cloves
- Lettuce (optional)
- Tomato (optional)
- Slices of provolone cheese (optional)
- Ciabatta Rolls

For the Sauce
- 1 teaspoon Sriracha
- 2 teaspoons minced Cilantro
- ¼ cup non-fat plain Greek yogurt

Directions:

1. Turn the grill on to medium-high heat.
2. Using a food processor, combine black beans, green peppers, garlic cloves, and red onion.
3. Puree the ingredients and pour it into a medium-sized bowl.
4. Crack in the eggs and mix everything together.
5. Toss in the roasted red peppers, cilantro, onion powder, chili powder and cumin.
6. Mix once more until everything is evenly distributed. Finally add panko before mixing a final time.

7. Mold the patties with hands and set them on the grill for 3 to 4 minutes on each side.
8. Once done, set on rolls and spoon sauce on top.

18 - Sriracha Veggie Fried Rice

Ingredients:

- 1 teaspoon minced ginger
- 2 teaspoons sesame oil
- 2 tablespoons peanut or vegetable oil
- 3 tablespoon low-sodium soy sauce
- 3 tablespoons Sriracha
- ½ cup frozen peas
- 3 cups cold leftover rice
- 1 minced garlic clove
- 2 scallions, white and green parts separated and thinly sliced
- 5 or 6 fresh shiitake mushrooms, stems removed and caps finely chopped
- Freshly ground black or white pepper to taste

Directions:

1. Get out a medium-sized skillet and heat it over a medium heat.
2. When a drop of water sizzles on the surface, pour in oil and coat the bottom.
3. Toss in the garlic, ginger, and scallion whites. Let them cook for 30 seconds then add the mushrooms and stir-fry for another minute.
4. Unclump the cold rice and toss into the skillet.
5. Ensure all clumps of rice are broken up using a spatula before adding the peas.
6. When rice turns golden after stir-frying, stir in sesame oil, Sriracha and soy sauce.
7. Pepper can be added to taste.
8. Serve in bowls and add scallion greens to garnish.

Delicious Sriracha Hot Sauce For A Spice Palate

Vegetarian And Salads

Delicious Sriracha Hot Sauce For A Spice Palate

19 - Spicy Mayo Fried Sole Sandwiches

Ingredients:

- ¼ cup extra virgin olive oil
- ½ cup bread-and-butter pickles
- 1 cup milk
- 1 cup loosely packed baby arugula
- 1 cup plain bread crumbs mixed with 1 teaspoon each coarse salt and freshly ground black pepper
- 1 lemon
- 1 baguette, cut in half lengthwise
- 3 fillets Dover sole, rinsed and patted dry with paper towels
- Spicy mayo

For the Spicy Mayo
- 1½ tablespoons ketchup
- 1½ tablespoons Sriracha
- 1 cup Vegenaise

Directions:

1. Heat up a large non-stick skillet and pour in olive oil.
2. In a bowl of milk, dip fish and dredge it in a bowl of bread crumbs.
3. Place the fish in the oil and let it cook for 2 minutes, flipping once for another 2 minutes.
4. When done, drain the fish on paper towels.
5. Squeeze a lemon half over the fish.
6. To make the mayo, combine all ingredients and mix well.
7. Once all that is done, spread the mayo on one side of bread and arrange the arugula and pickles evenly over top.
8. Slice the fish in half going lengthwise and arrange them on top of the arugula and pickles.
9. Place the other half of the baguette on top and cut into quarter pieces.
10. Plate with lemon wedges cut from the remaining half of lemon.

20 - Orange Broccoli and Tofu

Makes 4 servings

Ingredients:

- 1 teaspoon Sriracha
- 1 tablespoon cornstarch
- 1 tablespoon warm water
- 1 tablespoon finely grated orange zest
- 3 tablespoons rice vinegar
- 3 tablespoons honey
- 3 tablespoons vegetable oil
- ¼ cup low-sodium soy sauce
- ¾ cup orange juice
- 1 pound (450 g) broccoli florets
- 1 pound (450 g) firm tofu
- 3 minced garlic cloves

Directions:

1. Mix the cornstarch with warm water in a bowl.
2. Toss in rice vinegar, soy sauce, zest, orange juice and Sriracha. Set it aside.
3. Set the broccoli to steam for about 2 or 3 minutes. The color should be bright green with the outside still firm.
4. Prepare the tofu by draining and cut into cubes.
5. Get out a big non-stick pan and heat oil over a medium-high heat.
6. Toss the tofu into pan and let it all cook for about 6 to 8 minutes or until brown all over.
7. Toss in the garlic before cooking once more for about 30 seconds.
8. Now toss in the orange sauce and broccoli.
9. Stir everything together and cook until bubbles form in the sauce.
10. Bring the heat down and let it cook for another 2 or 3 minutes.
11. Pour into a bowl and eat with rice.

21 - Sriracha Tofu Skewers

Ingredients:

- 1 teaspoon arrowroot
- 3 tablespoons sesame seeds
- 4 tablespoons Sriracha
- 1 pound (450 g) extra firm tofu
- Zest of 1 lime
- 4-6 skewers (soaked)

Directions:

1. Set the oven 350°F (180°C) degrees.
2. Wrap up the tofu in a kitchen towel and flatten it between 2 plates. Keep it like that for an hour to drain all of the water.
3. Carefully cut the tofu into cubes and let them marinate in 4 tablespoons of the Sriracha for an hour.
4. Once done, set the tofu on a baking tray greased with oil and pour out the marinade into a saucepan.
5. Heat up the pan with arrowroot and take off immediately once it begins to boil. It should be thick at this point.
6. Brush the tofu with Sriracha and season with sesame seeds on top.
7. Skewer the tofu and let them bake for 40 minutes.
8. Once the tofu is firm and the coating appears sticky, they're done.
9. Use the zest of a lime to garnish.
10. Serve with coconut milk, lime zest, and coriander if desired.

22 - Thai Style Kale and Carrot Salad

Makes 4 servings

Ingredients:

- Pinch of salt
- Sesame seeds for garnish
- ½ teaspoon sesame oil
- ½ teaspoon extra virgin olive oil
- ½ teaspoon apple cider vinegar
- ½ teaspoon freshly grated ginger
- 1½ teaspoons Sriracha
- ½ tablespoon maple syrup
- 3 tablespoons creamy peanut butter
- 3 tablespoons almond milk
- 2 cups thinly sliced Tuscan kale
- 3 cups julienned carrot strings

Directions:

1. In a large bowl, mix the carrots and kale.
2. Add the rest of the ingredients in a small bowl, while leaving out the sesame seeds.
3. Use more milk if needed.
4. Pour the newly made sauce on the carrots and kale.
5. Toss everything together until the carrots and kale are coated.
6. Sprinkle sesame seeds on top and enjoy.

23 - Roasted Sriracha Cauliflower

Ingredients:

- ¼ teaspoon salt
- 1 tablespoon Sriracha
- 1 tablespoon olive oil
- 2 roughly chopped garlic cloves
- 1 chopped head of cauliflower

Directions:

1. Set the oven to 425°F (220°C).
2. Mix the chopped cauliflower and garlic with the Sriracha and olive oil.
3. Season with salt and bake for 20 minutes.

24 - Cauliflower Quinoa Medley with Sriracha Almond Sauce

Ingredients:

For the Quinoa
- ¼ teaspoon salt
- ½ teaspoon sesame oil
- ½ teaspoon Sriracha
- ½ cup quinoa
- 1 cup water

For the Cauliflower
- 1 small cauliflower or ½ head of large cauliflower
- ¼ teaspoon ginger powder
- 1 teaspoon sesame oil
- 1 teaspoon oil
- 1 teaspoon Sriracha

For the Greens
- A pinch of garlic powder and salt
- ½ teaspoon oil
- 2 tablespoons water
- 4-5 large leaves of collard greens

For the Almond Sriracha Sauce
- A generous pinch of salt
- ¼ teaspoon garlic powder
- ½ teaspoon sesame oil
- 1 teaspoon apple cider vinegar
- 1-2 teaspoons Sriracha to taste
- 2 teaspoons maple syrup
- 2 teaspoons extra virgin olive oil
- 2 teaspoons ginger minced
- 3 tablespoons coconut milk

- 3 tablespoons almond butter (or any other nut butter like peanut butter)

Directions:

1. Rinse the quinoa and place in pot with all the ingredients.
2. On medium heat, bring them to a boil then cook on a low-medium heat. The pot should be partially covered for 10 to 15 minutes.
3. Fluff up the quinoa and keep it ready.
4. Prepare the cauliflower by chopping it into little florets.
5. Combine all dressing ingredients in a bowl then add the cauliflower.
6. Season with salt before baking at a preheated 425°F (220°C) for 20 to 25 minutes.
7. Before using the collard greens, remove the tough ribs and chop the remaining greens chiffonade style.
8. Cook the collard greens while the cauliflower roasts.
9. Heat up the oil over medium heat in a pan.
10. Toss in the garlic, salt and collard greens and let them cook for a minute.
11. Now add in the water, mix everything, cover with a lid, and cook on a low-medium heat until all the ingredients look slightly wilted.
12. For the almond Sriracha sauce, combine all ingredients in a blender.
13. Blend everything together well, add salt and spice if desire.
14. To put everything together, set it all in a bowl and serve with a large portion of dressing, sesame seeds, and cilantro leaves.

25 - Sriracha Zest Roasted Chickpeas

Ingredients:

- ½ teaspoon sea salt
- 1 teaspoon lime juice
- 1 teaspoon grated lime zest
- 1½ teaspoons Sriracha
- 1 tablespoon fresh chopped cilantro
- 1 tablespoon extra virgin olive oil
- 1 can (15 ounces or 420 g) chickpeas

Directions:

1. Set the oven to 400°F (200°C) degrees.
2. Clean the chickpeas by rinsing them then draining the water. Pat them dry with paper towel.
3. Mix the olive oil, Sriracha, lime juice, and sea salt in a large bowl.
4. Toss in the chickpeas and mix to coat them.
5. Get out a baking sheet and line it with parchment paper.
6. Pour out the chickpeas on the pan so they're evenly spread.
7. Set the pan in the oven and cook for 35 to 40 minutes until crunchy.
8. Ensure to stir halfway through baking.
9. Afterwards, take them out and mix cilantro and lime zest.
10. Toss to coat the roasted chickpeas.
11. Let them cool then serve while warm.

Soups And Stews

Delicious Sriracha Hot Sauce For A Spice Palate

26 - Sriracha Honey Beef Stew

Ingredients:

- ½ teaspoon Sriracha, or more to taste
- 2 teaspoons rice vinegar
- 2 tablespoons oil (olive, rice bran, vegetable, etc.)
- 3 tablespoons honey
- ¼ cup low-sodium soy sauce
- ¼ cup oyster-flavored sauce
- 1 cup dried mushrooms
- 14-ounces (390 g) bag frozen pearl onions, defrosted
- 2 cups all-purpose flour
- 2 pounds (900 g) stew beef
- 1-inch (2.5 cm) piece of peeled ginger root
- 1 medium diced red onion
- 3 peeled and sliced garlic cloves
- 4 medium peeled and sliced carrots of ½-inch (1.25 cm) thickness
- Salt and black pepper to taste

Directions:

1. In a 2-cup measuring container, set the mushrooms inside and fill up with water.
2. Place the cup in the microwave and cook it for 3 minutes. Take out and set off to the side.
3. Ensure the beef is cut up into chunks before drying off using a few paper towels.
4. Pour the flour into a large mixing bowl.
5. Using a slow cooker or non-stick frying pan, pour in the oil and heat it.
6. Mix the beef in with the flour until it is coated. Then lay the beef in the oil and brown it.
7. After all beef is brown, put it into a 5 or 6-quart (5 to 6 L) slow cooker.

8. Gently add in the rice vinegar, oyster sauce, soy sauce, carrots, onion, ginger and garlic and stir everything in.
9. Take the mushrooms and pour the water with a strainer into another cup. Add this cup to the slow cooker.
10. Set the mushrooms aside to be used elsewhere.
11. Cover up the slow cooker to cook for 4 hours on low.
12. After 4 hours, add the Sriracha, honey and onions to cook for another ½ hour.
13. Add salt and pepper to taste.
14. Take out the vegetables and beef from the cooker and place them in a large bowl.
15. The remaining sauce should be poured into a saucepan on the stove.
16. Set the heat to a medium-high heat and let it reduce to about half the original quantity which should take about 10 minutes.
17. At this point, the sauce should be thick and have a honey sheen.
18. Now pour the thickened sauce over all the vegetables and meat and mix everything.
19. Serve while still hot with noodles or rice.

27 - Egg with Mushroom Shrimp Noodle Soup

Makes 4 servings

Ingredients:

- 1 tablespoon fresh ginger, minced
- 1 tablespoon fish sauce
- 1 tablespoon rice vinegar
- 2 tablespoons low-sodium soy sauce
- 2 tablespoons sesame oil
- 8 ounces (224 g) rice noodles
- 12 ounces (360 ml) mushrooms, cleaned and sliced
- 2 cups cooked shrimp, room temperature
- 6 cups low-sodium chicken stock
- 1 thinly sliced jalapeño
- 4 fried (or poached) eggs
- 2 limes, cut into wedges
- 2 minced garlic cloves
- 3 sliced green onions
- Sriracha for serving
- Chopped cilantro for serving (optional)

Directions:

1. Get out a shallow dish and place the rice noodles in the bowl.
2. Cover with room temperature water and set to the side.
3. For the soup, pour sesame oil in a large soup pot and heat over a medium heat.
4. Toss the mushrooms, but don't stir for 3 minutes. Stir once then let sit for 3 minutes.
5. Now combine with the garlic and ginger and stir everything together.
6. Cook the mix for 30 seconds and then add the jalapeño and green onions.

7. Give the mix one more minute to cook and then add the chicken stock.
8. Turn up the heat to a boil, and then add the shrimp after it boils.
9. Drain the water from the rice noodles and toss in the soup.
10. Now drop in the soy sauce, fish sauce, and rice vinegar.
11. Begin cooking the eggs.
12. After the shrimp cooks thoroughly and the noodles feel soft, take off the soup from the heat and serve with an egg in each bowl.
13. Garnished with the cilantro, Sriracha, and lime on top.

28 - Coconut Chicken Soup

Ingredients:

- 1 teaspoon sugar
- 1 tablespoon fish sauce
- 5 kaffir lime leaves or 1 tablespoon lime zest and $1/8$ cup lime juice
- 4 ounces (112 g) shiitake mushrooms, stemmed, caps cut into bite-size pieces
- 6 ounces (168 g) boneless, skinless chicken breasts, cut into 1-inch (2.5 cm) pieces
- 6 ounces (168 g) coconut milk
- 3 cups low-sodium chicken stock
- 1 piece ginger, peeled
- Sriracha, cilantro leaves, and lime wedges (for serving)

Directions:

1. Gently smash up the ginger using a knife. In a saucepan, combine ginger, lime leaves, and stock. Bring it all to a boil, then take it down to a simmer for about 8 to 10 minutes.
2. Pour the stock through a strainer and into a clean saucepan.
3. Throw out any leftover solids.
4. Toss in the chicken and bring everything to a boil once more.
5. Take the heat down, toss in the mushrooms, and let it all simmer while skimming when needed.
6. Once the chicken is thoroughly cooked and the mushrooms appear soft, add the coconut milk, fish sauce, and sugar.
7. Serve the soup in bowls then top with Sriracha, cilantro, and lime wedges.

29 - Sriracha Black Bean Soup

Ingredients:

- ½ teaspoon chipotle chili powder
- ½ teaspoon chili powder
- ½ teaspoon salt
- 1 teaspoon pimento (smoked paprika)
- 1 teaspoon to 2 tablespoons Sriracha sauce
- 2 teaspoons Worcestershire sauce
- 1 tablespoon maple syrup
- 1 tablespoon olive oil
- 2 tablespoons BBQ sauce
- 2 tablespoons sour cream, for garnish
- ¼ cup chopped fresh cilantro (save some for garnish)
- 1 cup pepper jack cheese or white cheddar for garnish
- 1 cup diced onion (about ½ of a large onion)
- 3 cans black beans (15 ½-ounce or 465 ml), drained but not rinsed
- 2 cups chicken stock (can substitute with vegetable broth)
- 2 minced garlic cloves
- 2 seeded, peeled and finely chopped tomatoes or one 15 ounce (450 ml) can crushed tomatoes
- 4 finely chopped slices regular or 2 slices thick uncooked bacon (or vegetarian substitute)
- Salt and freshly ground black pepper

Directions:

1. Using a large stock pot, pour in the olive oil and heat.
2. When it simmers, toss in bacon pieces.
3. Add onions once the bacon fat renders.
4. Stir the onions and bacon together until the onions appear translucent. Move them to the side before tilting the pot so the fat slides to the other side.
5. Now toss in the salt, chili powders and paprika to the fat and mix it until a paste forms.

6. Stir in the garlic and mix thoroughly, covering all the vegetables in the fat.
7. Now pour in the stock and raise the heat to a medium-high temperature.
8. Toss in the Sriracha, Worcestershire sauce, maple syrup, BBQ sauce, black beans and tomatoes. Mix all components together until the soup boils.
9. Take the heat down to a simmer and cook partially for 15 minutes.
10. Add salt and pepper to taste.
11. Finally, add the cilantro and stir. Keep a little out for garnish.
12. If a smoother, thicker soup is desired, mash the soup or run it through an immersion blender. Half of the beans should remain intact.
13. Pour soup into bowls, top with sour cream and season with cheese and cilantro.

30 - Sriracha Beef Stew

Ingredients:

- 2 teaspoons ginger
- 4 tablespoons Sriracha
- ¼ cup sesame seeds
- 2 pounds (900 g) stew beef
- 1 chopped red bell pepper
- 1 chopped green bell pepper
- 1 chopped sweet onion
- 3 minced garlic cloves

Directions:

1. In a slow cooker, add vegetables, stew beef and Sriracha.
2. Stir ingredients together so all looks evenly spread, then cover the pot and let it all cook on a low heat for 6 to 8 hours.

31 - Sriracha Garlic Butternut Squash & Pumpkin Soup

Ingredients:

- 1 tablespoon extra virgin olive oil
- 1 tablespoon Sriracha
- ½ cup 1% milk
- ½ cup half-n-half cream
- 1 cup of canned pumpkin puree
- 1 pound (450 g) of peeled and seeded butternut squash, cut into ½-inch (1.25 cm) chunks
- 4 cups of vegetable broth
- ½ chopped sweet onion
- 2 chopped stalks of celery
- 3 large peeled and chopped garlic cloves
- Sea salt and freshly ground pepper to taste

Directions:

1. Get out a large pot and heat the oil over a medium heat.
2. Toss in the onions and celery. Sauté everything while stirring often.
3. Reduce the heat before adding garlic.
4. Cook and stir for another 2 minutes then toss in the squash. Cook altogether 3 to 4 minutes.
5. Now turn up the heat and add the vegetable broth.
6. Next add the pumpkin and mix everything together thoroughly before bringing the mixture to a boil.
7. Let it simmer for 20 to 25 minutes on low heat until the squash is soft. This can be checked using a fork to pierce the squash.
8. Turn off the heat completely and allow it to cool.
9. Next pour in the milk and half and half then puree the mixture with an immersion blender.
10. Alternatively, the soup can also be poured into a blender and pureed.

11. Once blended, sprinkle salt and pepper to desired amount and serve.

Desserts

Delicious Sriracha Hot Sauce For A Spice Palate

32 - Sriracha Choco Popsicles

Makes 4 servings

Ingredients:

- ½ teaspoon vanilla extract
- 1 teaspoon Sriracha
- ½ tablespoon unsalted butter
- 1 tablespoon cornstarch
- 1½ tablespoons cocoa powder
- 2 tablespoons semisweet chocolate chips or chopped semisweet chocolate
- ⅓ cup sugar
- 1¼ cups whole milk
- Pinch of salt

Directions:

1. Using very low heat, melt the chocolate in a medium sized saucepan. Let it melt while stirring constantly until completely smooth.
2. Add sugar, cocoa powder, salt, cornstarch, milk, and Sriracha to the chocolate.
3. Turn up the heat to medium and continue to stir often. The mixture should cook for another 5 to 10 minutes until thick.
4. Turn off the heat and toss in the vanilla and butter.
5. Mix everything until it's fully combined. Let it cool and then spoon the mixture into popsicle molds.
6. Put the molds in the freezer for 30 minutes.
7. Once partially frozen, take out and place the popsicle sticks into the molds.
8. Put them back into the freezer until fully solid.

33 - Crunchy Pecan Sriracha Brownies

Makes about 34 Brownies

Ingredients:

For the Brittle
- 1½ teaspoons Sriracha
- 1 tablespoon butter
- ⅓ cup granulated sugar
- ½ cup chopped pecans

For the Brownies
- ¾ teaspoon salt
- 2 teaspoons vanilla extract
- 4 tablespoons melted unsalted butter
- ⅓ cup cocoa powder
- 4 ounces (112 g) chopped bittersweet chocolate
- 4 ounces (112 g) bittersweet chocolate
- ½ cup plus 2 tablespoons boiling water
- ½ cup plus 2 tablespoons vegetable oil
- 1¾ cups all-purpose flour
- 2½ cups granulated sugar
- 2 large eggs
- 2 egg yolks

Directions:

1. Get out a 9 x 13-inch (22.5 x 32.5 cm) baking pan and set the oven to 350°F (180°C).
2. Coat the pan with non-stick cooking spray and set it off to the side for the brownie batter.
3. Get out a baking sheet and line it with foil. Set it aside for the brittle.
4. Begin by making the brittle. Set a medium skillet on the stove and toss in the pecans, ⅓ cup granulated sugar, and 1 tablespoon of butter.

5. Let them cook over a medium heat while continuously stirring as the sugar melts.
6. Turn the heat down to a low heat.
7. Toss in the Sriracha and cook until the sugar turns a golden color.
8. Pour the liquid brittle onto the lined baking sheet and let it cool.
9. Next tackle the brownies. Combine cocoa powder and boiling water until the mix is smooth.
10. Mix in the 4 ounces of chocolate until it melts.
11. Next add the melted butter and oil. Whisk it all together.
12. Combine eggs, yolks, and vanilla by mixing into the batter then add in sugar, flour and salt. Mix everything together.
13. Gently fold in the chopped chocolate.
14. Get out the greased brownie pan and pour the batter in. Put it in the oven and bake.
15. After 15 minutes, take out of oven and distribute crushed brittle evenly over top. Press it all over and down into the brownie batter.
16. Put the pan back in the oven for 15 more minutes.
17. Take out once done and let it cool.
18. Finally, cut the brownies into bars.

34 - Lime Sriracha Donuts

Makes about 18 to 20 donuts

Ingredients:
For the Donuts:

- ½ teaspoon salt
- 1 tablespoon baking powder
- 2 tablespoons lime zest
- ⅓ cup lime juice, freshly squeezed
- ½ cup heavy cream
- ½ cup Sriracha
- ½ cup canola oil
- 1 cup unsalted butter, softened
- 1 cup white sugar, granulated
- 2 large eggs
- 3½ cups all-purpose flour

For the Glaze
- ¼ cup heavy cream
- ¼ cup lime juice, freshly squeezed
- 1½ cup powdered sugar

Directions:

1. Set the oven to 350°F (180°C).
2. Get out a donut pan with 6 cavities and grease it. Set it to the side.
3. Mix the butter and sugar together with mixer. Use a paddle attachment for this.
4. Next toss in the cream and oil and mix together.
5. Carefully pour in the flour, salt, and baking powder while adding in the Sriracha and lime juice, one and then the other.
6. Add the zest and fold the dough until the batter is evenly mixed.
7. Get out a piping bag and fill it with batter.
8. Carefully pipe the batter into the cavities of the donut pan.
9. Put it in the oven and bake for about 16 minutes. The donuts will be golden brown when they're done.
10. Take them out and let them cool.
11. To make the glaze, mix the powdered sugar, heavy cream, and lime juice together until the batter is smooth.
12. After the donuts have cooled, take them out of the mold and set them on the cooling rack.
13. Spoon the glaze over the top and serve them.

35 - Sriracha Ice Cream Sandwich Delight

Ingredients:

For the Cookies
- ¼ teaspoon salt
- ½ teaspoon baking soda
- 1 teaspoon pure vanilla extract
- ⅛ to ¼ cup Sriracha
- ¼ cup chocolate chunks
- ½ cup light brown sugar
- ½ cup granulated white sugar
- ¾ cup unsalted butter, room temperature
- ¾ cup peanut butter (crunchy)
- 2 cups all-purpose flour
- 2 large eggs

For the Ice Cream
- ¾ cup shredded coconut
- 1 bunch of Thai basil
- 1 carton of vanilla bean ice cream

Directions:

1. Mix all the cookie ingredients then add the Sriracha sauce last.
2. On parchment paper and a baking sheet, spread the shredded coconut and bake at 385°F (195°C) for 15 minutes until golden brown.
3. Set aside to cool off.
4. Softened the ice cream by folding it a few times on a flat solid surface.
5. Add finely chopped up basil and whip the mixture. Once done, place in freezer to set.
6. Dividing the cookie dough into quarters, roll each quarter into a ball and flatten into patties.
7. Use a knife to form grid patterns on the surface.

8. Place the patties on a baking sheet with parchment paper and bake in the oven at 350°F (180°C) for 10 to 12 minutes or until the edges become lightly brown.
9. Once done, let the cookies cool on a wire rack. If baking ahead of time, they may be stored at room temperature for up to a week or in the freezer for a longer period.
10. Once the cookies have cooled, soften the ice cream and add a scoop on top of one of the cookies.
11. Top it off with another cookie and roll the exposed ice cream sides over the toasted coconut.
12. Repeat this procedure for the second sandwich.
13. Serve cold and enjoy!

36 - Chocolate Bite Ice Cream

Makes 4 servings

Ingredients:

- ½ teaspoon ground cinnamon
- 2 teaspoon Sriracha
- 2½ tablespoons maple syrup
- 3 tablespoons cocoa powder
- 1 can full-fat coconut milk

Directions:

1. In a small bowl, combine the cocoa powder, cinnamon, Sriracha, and maple syrup.
2. Whisk it until it looks clumpy.
3. Pour the coconut milk slowly into the mixture ensuring it remains smooth.
4. Once the coconut milk has been added and mixed, set the bowl in the freezer and let it cool for 25 minutes.

5. As soon as it's done, pour the mixture into an ice cream maker and let it freeze entirely.

37 - Crispy Sriracha Peach Bake

Ingredients:

- ½ teaspoon cinnamon
- 1 teaspoon cornstarch
- 1 tablespoon Sriracha
- 2 tablespoons honey
- 3 pounds (1,350 g) or 4-6 fresh peaches

For the crumble topping

- ½ teaspoon salt
- ½ cup or 1 stick butter
- ½ cup brown sugar
- 1 cup rolled oats
- 1 cup all-purpose flour

Directions:

1. Mix the Sriracha, honey and cinnamon in a small bowl.
2. Cut up the peaches into small pieces and toss into the mixture. Ensure the peach pieces are coated.
3. Mix in the cornstarch and toss again.
4. In another bowl, mix the brown sugar, salt, flour and oats until evenly distributed.
5. Mix in the butter to make a crumbly sand-like paste. Use your hands if necessary.
6. In an 8 x 8 inch (20 x 20 cm) baking dish, cover the bottom with the coated peach pieces. Add the oat mixture on top of the peaches.
7. Place the baking dish in the oven and bake at 375°F (190°C) until golden brown about 30 minutes. The fruit should be bubbling up at this point.
8. Remove from the oven.
9. Serve either hot or cold.

38 - Spiced Lattice Apple Pie

Makes 4 servings

Ingredients:

- Crust for 2-crust pie
- ¼ teaspoon cloves
- 1 teaspoon cinnamon
- 1½ teaspoons Sriracha
- ¼ cup water
- ½ cup unsalted butter
- 3 tablespoons all-purpose flour
- ½ cup white sugar
- ½ cup brown sugar
- 8 to 10 large peeled, cored and sliced apples

Directions:

1. In a sauce pan, melt the butter over medium heat.

2. Add in water, Sriracha, cinnamon, sugars and flour. Turn up the heat to a boil. Once boiling, bring it down to a simmer for about 5 minutes.
3. Place the bottom crust in a pan and carefully brush it with melted butter. Top with sugar.
4. Combine the sugar mix with the apple and pour the mix into the crust. Cover up the apples with the lattice crust and sprinkle sugar and cinnamon on top.
5. Put the pie in the oven and bake for 15 minutes at 425°F (230°C).
6. Bring the temperature down to 350°F (180°C) and let it bake for another 35 to 40 minutes.
7. Take out once the apples look golden.
8. If you want to use pears instead of apples, toss in 1 cup chopped pecans and 1 cup raisins that have been soaked in rum.

Delicious Sriracha Hot Sauce For A Spice Palate

Specialty Sauces

Delicious Sriracha Hot Sauce For A Spice Palate

39 - Mayonnaise with Sriracha

Ingredients:

- ¼ teaspoon granulated garlic
- 1 tablespoon ketchup
- 2 tablespoons Sriracha sauce
- ½ cup prepared mayonnaise

Directions:

1. Mix all ingredients in a bowl then use as condiment for burgers or sandwiches of your choice.
2. Should be used immediately or may be stored in refrigerator for up to 2 days in an airtight container.

40 - Creamy Lime Sriracha Dip

Ingredients:

- ¼ teaspoon low-sodium soy sauce
- 1 teaspoon lemon or lime juice
- 1 tablespoon Sriracha
- 3 tablespoons mayonnaise

Directions:

1. Mix all ingredients in a bowl until smooth.
2. Serve with a favorite cracker or raw vegetable.

41 - Asian Bean Dip

Ingredients:

- ½ teaspoon curry powder
- 1 teaspoon sesame oil
- 2 teaspoons low-sodium soy sauce (or to taste)
- 1 tablespoon olive oil
- 1 tablespoon lime juice
- 2 tablespoons Sriracha
- ¼ cup of water
- 1 x 15-ounce (420 g) can of white beans
- 1 large garlic clove
- Crackers or fried crispy bread

Directions:

1. Ensure the white beans are rinsed before using.
2. Mix all ingredients in a blender and blend until all smooth.
3. Eat with crackers or on toast.

Delicious Sriracha Hot Sauce For A Spice Palate

Drinks

Delicious Sriracha Hot Sauce For A Spice Palate

42 - Sriracha Bloody Mary

Ingredients:

- ¼ teaspoon freshly grated Horseradish
- ½ ounce fresh Lemon Juice
- 2 ounces (60 ml) vodka
- 4 ounces (120 ml) tomato juice
- 2 pinches celery salt
- 2 dashes Worcestershire sauce
- 3 dashes Sriracha

Directions:

1. Pour all ingredients into a mixing glass.
2. Add a few ice cubes, then roll the glass.
3. Do not shake.
4. Strain into a glass and garnish.

43 - Sriracha Strawberry Margarita

Ingredients:

- ½ teaspoon Sriracha
- 1 tablespoon agave nectar
- ¼ cup Cointreau (or other orange flavored liquor)
- ½ cup tequila
- 2 cups strawberries, hulled and chopped
- 2 cups ice

Directions:

1. Combine all ingredients in a blender and blend until mixture is smooth.
2. Serve in a sugar-rimmed margarita glass.

44 - Spicy Pineapple Paradise

Ingredients:

- ¼ teaspoon Sriracha
- ¾ ounce (22.5 ml) simple syrup
- 2 ounces (60 ml) pineapple juice
- 3 ounces (90 ml) vodka
- 10 cilantro leaves

Directions:

1. Mix everything in a shaker. Be sure there's ice in it.
2. Shake all together then strain into a rocks glass filled with fresh ice.
3. Use a lime wedge for garnish.

45 - Mango Sriracha Shots

Ingredients:

- 1 teaspoon Sriracha
- ¼ cup whiskey
- ⅓ cup corn syrup
- ¾ cup ripe mango puree
- 2 cups ice cubes
- Juice of 1 lime

Directions:

1. Pour all ingredients into a shaker and mix together for 3 to 5 minutes.
2. Get out the shot glasses and pour Sriracha and mango mix into each glass.
3. Serve and enjoy.

46 - Ginger Sriracha Lime Cocktail

Makes 4 servings

Ingredients:

- 6 shots (9 ounces or 270 ml) of vodka
- 24 ounces (720 ml) of ginger ale
- Juice from 2 large limes
- 32 drops of Sriracha
- Ice cubes and 1 lemon, sliced in wedges for serving

Directions:

1. Mix all ingredients with ice in a pitcher.
2. Serve the drink in a highball glass with extra ice and use a lemon wedge as garnish.

Thank You

If you enjoyed the recipes, please consider leaving a review of the book. Good reviews encourage an author to write as well as help books to sell. Good reviews can be just a few short sentences describing what you liked about the book. If you could spend 30 seconds writing a review, I would appreciate it. You can review this title right now at your favorite retailer.

Other Books by Brianne Heaton

- 51 Dump Cake Recipes: Scrumptious Dump Cake Desserts To Satisfy Your Sweet Tooth

- 56 Breakfast Sandwich Recipes: Irresistible Sandwich Ideas to Kickstart Your Morning

- 50 Holiday Dessert Recipes: Delectable Dessert Ideas For The Christmas Holidays And Other Special Occasions

- 51 Easter Dessert Ideas: Scrumptious Easter Recipes For Any Occasion

Get the latest update on new releases from the author at:

https://www.brianneheaton.com/newsletter

About the Author – Brianne Heaton

Brianne Heaton started off collecting recipes that her family and friends enjoyed. After receiving many requests for copies of the recipes, she decided to share them by writing recipes books that everyone would appreciate.

Visit Brianne's website at:

https://www.brianneheaton.com/

Connect with Brianne Heaton

I really appreciate you reading my book! Here are my social media contact information:

Friend me on Facebook: https://www.facebook.com/BrianneHeatonRecipeBooks/

Follow me on Twitter: https://twitter.com/brianneheaton

Check me out on Goodreads: https://www.goodreads.com/author/show/8121938.Brianne_Heaton

Subscribe to my newsletter: https://www.brianneheaton.com/newsletter/

Visit my website: https://www.brianneheaton.com/

www.ingramcontent.com/pod-product-compliance
Lightning Source LLC
Chambersburg PA
CBHW061802070526
44586CB00023B/2679